The War in The Gulf was first published in The Wolf.

May The First was originally written and performed for BBC Five Live.

For Mr. Cotter, Mrs McIness, Mr. Sime, and Mr. Wilmott.

And for Archie MacDonald and John and Micheal Russell who will remember these names.

'All the poets they studied rules of verse.
And those ladies they rolled their eyes.'

The Velvet Underground, Sweet Jane

Algorithms Ate My Lunch
Brussels, December 2008

We worked in Rembrandt's studio
Painting skies at his command
While the Master made the sunlight
The faces and the hands

Or else in Blacksmiths' forges
Shoeing stallions and mares
The dignity of labour
Answering our hopes and prayers

We are not artists now nor artisans
As we once were in days gone by
But ciphers now subtracted
From where the numbers never lie

Brave Little Soldier
Ixelles, December 2020

I see you from my window
In your tin can every night
You've done nothing wrong today
And that makes everything all right

You're a brave little soldier
But oh what have you done
With your Masters and Max Maras
And your pretty pearl encrusted gun

I see you at the check-in
Off again to join the battle
You've taken your best lingerie
And so many pills you rattle

You're a brave little soldier
But oh what have you done
You've more degrees than a thermometer
But there's not a single bullet in that gun

Dontbai
Dubai, February 2006

In shopping malls with prayer rooms
The soft porn hides its nipples
Whilst Mammon shoes the pretty feet
Of fashionista's cripples
Suicidal Hindus cannot prick the collective conscience
Living nightmares building dream homes
Above the height of nonsense
Souks of gold from God knows where washed clean by unseen hands
As Sim City on testosterone rises from the sand
Here youth has lost its innocence and turned to rape and pillage
To build media a city and knowledge just a village

Finally
Ixelles, November 2021

I finally wrote a love song
After all these years
Now there's no more ink to spill
And just a few last tears
Now the book is written
Now I've closed the page
Yes there is some anger left
But at least there's no more rage

You are all the books I bought
And didn't ever read
You are all the things I wanted
And didn't ever need

These days it seems to hurt too much
To ever try and think
Now all the knowledge in the world
Has turned to disappearing ink
We are both so far away now
From what either would prefer
I am just not him now
And you are just not her

You are the way that you still look at me
Unsurprised no mater what
You are the door that has been long since closed
But that someone forgot to lock

GPS
Ixelles, December 2020

The mobile's dead
And I'm not well
A ring tone plays inside my head
But no-one's face here rings a bell

I had an itch for scratching
So I took off for twenty years
To find a hill of happiness
Above a vale of tears

Somewhere to fix a smile in place
To put on one last one-man show
Where only me and my black dog
Will ever know it is not so

How Do You Sleep
Doha, May 2010

Beyond the umpteenth parallel
Drawn by your fathers on our land
Hundreds die in slavery
As billions bubble from the sand
We need do no more than help ourselves
To all the toys and trinkets
We can ever buy in Paradise
Or we will ever need in Hell
In Business Class the afterlife is comfortable
We need not question how or why
Nor judge the flatness of the beds
Upon which we have learned to lie

Left To Our Own Devices
Ixelles, June 2020

It's emojis and hashtags and living the dream
It's the howl in the meme of Munch and The Scream
It's the grid and the post and the snap and the view
It's the screen that reflects the me in the you
It's the dopamine fix that's getting us high
Knowing we are the truth and they are the lie
It's every day we keep writing the song
About us being right and them being wrong
It's every night we keep playing the game
About who are the mad and who are the sane
It's everything smart things have made us become
Echoes among the deaf and the dumb

Love In The Time Of Corona
Brussels, March 2020

Christmas Eve on Friday Morning
Auld Lang Sine as midnight tolls
Panic buying going viral
Self isolating toilet rolls
Children buying chocolate rabbits
Japanese girls eating frites
Empty busses moving
Homeless alone on deserted streets
Making love and making coffee
Naked in our hopes and dreams
Together for a month of Sundays
Knowing God alone knows what it means

May The First
Warsaw, May 2004

European Christian Muslim Jew
May the first at last bring peace to you
From The Vistula to Scotland's Shores
Let it today consign our wars
To History where they belong
And trust its union makes us strong
Today let us begin to tolerate
To value and appreciate
That in the difference of our skins and tongues
We find a richness that becomes
A quality to celebrate
In each and every European State

Pointless
Ixelles, December 2020

Mary Magdalene's an inch offside with her first touch on the cross
Jesus saves St Peter's penalty then hoofs a long ball out the box
He says he wants me for a sunbeam and he offers me a quarter
But for now I'll keep my clean sheet for the Devil and his daughter
Its as pointless as a broken pencil or a bottomless Cornetto
As pointless as a fencing mask or Cortazar's Silent Concerto

I'm in with Marx and Engels and we've put it all on red
And Adam Smith looks mortified but he's already dead
I'm looking round the room but there's no sucker I can see
Then Yanis ups and leaves so I guess that makes it me
Its as pointless as s shaven grizzly bear or a bipolar emoji
As you know I'll always love you or an alarm call for a baby

Frieda says that history books repeat themselves and who am I to disagree
While Bing and Bob and Cliff gift wrap presents for the tree
Behind the VIP bar there's bills here to be settled
But I'm all out of credit and the Milky Bars have melted
Its as pointless as a joke without a punchline or a pack of toothless dogs
As one hand clapping in an empty room or one of a pair of clogs

Steve Jobs tells Mahatma Ghandi the one about the Dali Lama's pizza
The girl made one with everything in order to complete her
But she and I we both knew then it would only ever end in tears
Although we thought that maybe somehow we might last a few more years.
Its as pointless as a teardrop or a prequel you've not seen
As a pothole on the one track road that takes you back to where you've been

Prozac
Shropshire, January 2003

It isn't drink or drugs
It's prescription medication
The all important difference
Between levity and levitation
It's supposed to help my understanding
Of what you like to call your credo
But it just makes the world seem flat to me
And it's ruined my libido

Benecol
Shropshire, January 2003

We went to see Relate today
To talk about our issues
Over a mug of Nescafe
And a box of man sized tissues
We couldn't find the way at first
Which rather said it all
About how life came to overwhelm us
And shrink us down so small
On a poster at a junction
It said to watch your heart
But it didn't mention anywhere
That that's the hardest part

Rock & Roll
Liverpool, February 2020

It's good for the body
And it's good for the soul
The Blues had a baby
That they called Rock & Roll
It's good for the mind
And it's good for the heart
Some call it boogie
And some call it art
In New York and London
In Hamburg and Malmo
It's one two three four
And hey ho and let's go
Its the food of lost love
Of heartache and pain
That lump in the throat
That chorus again
An affirmation of life
The why not in the why
It won't go away
And it's not going to die

Say Hello
Ixelles, December 2020

In the morning buying bread
It could well stop you dropping dead
As you hurry on your way
Talk to people every day
On the bus or when you cross the street
Say hello to those you meet
Running to another meeting
Take time out for a simple greeting
On the metro or the tram
Put away your Instagram
Lifeanddeath is not a hashtag
You won't find it gift wrapped in a shopping bag
It's all around us every day
It's what we do and what we say
It's every face we don't yet know
It's every time we say hello

Song for K
Brussels, March 2020

And so I rowed you to the shore
To let you find your promised land
Then turning once more to the sea
The compass slipped out of my hand

As others come and others go
This is the only thing I know

Round sinking ship and fragile load
My friends the gulls took wing to fly
Then a voice against the storm arose
Women and their children first she cried

As storms come and as storms go
This is the only thing I know

Young sharks smell blood
And save for an albatross alone
I find it's better not to swim
But to trust the tide to take me home

As tides come and as tides go
This is the only thing I know

Not as a lover but a friend
I wake now in your promised land
To share the best part of the day
To walk you home and take your hand

As mornings come and evenings go
This is the only thing I know

The Hotel Lucky
Sopot, September 2003

We shall go together
To where you have been before
And you shall feed me love there
As we walk upon the shore
I shall tell you stories
About things you have not seen
And we shall sing a song there
About a yellow submarine
We shall step down from the train
And I shall take your hand
And at The Hotel Lucky
We shall dance upon the sand

The Last Chance Saloon
Dubai, November 2005

Irishmen and Dutch girls drinking Tiger Beer
Is as close to integration as it ever gets in here
Tipsy English teachers practise provocation
A solitary Indian awaits reincarnation
Lebanese smoke Gauloises
Philipina serve them Scotch
Serbians play football
Egyptians sit and watch
The jukebox spins its pop songs
Australians sing along
The Finnish cellphone silent
The Polish girl Long gone

The War In The Gulf
London, March 2003

The right word's worth more than a thousand TV channels
As the lily stands ungilded by their pundits and their panels
It speaks of what we see ourselves unspun before our eyes
Of Empires now prostrated before their ruined prize
A million more and marching fit to raise the roof
Until their bloody war becomes the first casualty of truth

Tomorrow's Stars
London, June 2003

Rumbling Home to Bedfordshire
Beneath the sulphur light
The Evening Standard on your knee
Says everything will be all right
Mercury is retrograde
But Scorpio's ascendent
So put off signing contracts
And take good care of your dependants
Avoid arguments with colleagues
True love is waiting to be found
For what is written in the stars above
Is often clearest underground

Trigger Warning
Ixelles, February 2022

Yes it does need to be said
But before the Riot Act is read
For now slip on the safety catch
Pour a glass and sit down and relax
Whatever sparked such fearsome ire
There's no returning friendly fire
Some days it's good to hold your tongue
Sometimes it's best to play along
To count to ten, to bide your time
To step back from the firing line
To sleep on it to calibrate
Lest misunderstandings escalate

Uncertainty
Brussels, November 2015

When a certain kind of person
Turns a certain kind of age
And a certain kind of lover
Turns a certain kind of page
It's a moment fraught with danger
And a certain kind of choice
An uncertain kind of strangeness
Or a certain strangers voice
Call it wisdom call it knowledge
It's a question of degree
And a certain understanding
That what will be will be
So mark your book of learning
And join me at the edge
And maybe we will speak then
Of all that's in our hearts and heads
One will strike the flame there
And one will set the fire
In its ashes there are memories
But in its warmth there is desire

Warsawa
Warsaw, June 2003

Beneath a milk white monument
To a slaughtered secret army
Masters of the universe
Masticate on calamari
The waitress in her jet black hot pants
Takes away their breath
In the shadow of the valley of her father's father's death
An old soldier gathers boxes of bruised raspberries and plums
Bt the market's silent testament
To what he has not yet become
Beneath the dislocated darkness
Love is sold or dissipated
Its violence now violation
Among the violated
All that we have ever known is handed down as new
As all that we are certain of
And all that we can do
But which of us is buying what
And which of us is selling
The then time of our knowledge
Or the now time of its telling

With Apologies To Philip Larkin
Kirkcudbright, March, 2001

They tuck you up your mum and dad
In mortgaged guilt and spent repentance
Until the words that never crossed their lips
Become your solitary life sentence
Some nights they drink sweet sherry
And they share a cigarette
As they choke upon their feelings
And they swallow their regrets
Doing much as you do now
Nursing your resentments
Yet both today are dead and buried
And can no more excuse your disappointments

With thanks to Fabrizio Nicolucci (Design & Art Direction)
and Kardama Pedalbxl (Photography).

Fist Published in May 2022 by **Paragon Publishing**

ISBN 978-1-78222-928-5

www.ingramcontent.com/pod-product-compliance
Lightning Source LLC
Chambersburg PA
CBHW070802050426
42452CB00012B/2460

9781782229285